AMERICAN
FORESTS

WILLIAM K SMITHEY

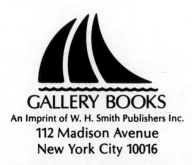

GALLERY BOOKS
An Imprint of W. H. Smith Publishers Inc.
112 Madison Avenue
New York City 10016

Text
William K. Smithey

Editorial
Gill Waugh

Design
Clive Dorman

Production
Ruth Arthur
David Proffit
Sally Connolly
Andrew Whitelaw

Jacket Design
Claire Leighton

Commissioning Editor
Andrew Preston

Director of Production
Gerald Hughes

Publishing Assistant
Edward Doling

Director of Publishing
David Gibbon

Photography
Planet Earth Pictures:
Brian Alker 29 *bottom*; Rob Beighton 11; Ron Bohr 6 *top*, 22 *bottom*;
Jim Brandenburg 13 *bottom*, 25, Franz J. Camenzind 12 *top*, 13 *top*,
29 *center and top*; Mary Clay 6 *bottom*, 7 *bottom*, 20 *bottom left and
top*, 22 *top*; Richard Coomber 30; John Downer 15 *bottom*; D. Robert
Franz 7 *top left*, 18 *bottom*, 19 *bottom right*, 23; Dr. Peter Gasson 26
top; Robert A Juriet front cover, 4-5, 20 *bottom right*, 31 *top*; Kenneth
Lucas 10, 26 *bottom*; Steve Nicholls 15 *top*; Doug Perrine 28; David
Phillips 7 *top right*; David A. Ponton 8 *top*, 14, 16, 24, 27 *top*; David E.
Rowley back cover, 17, 27 *bottom*, 31 *bottom*; Gilbert van
Ryckevorsel 9; William K. Smithey 32; Nigel Tucker 18-19 *top*, 19
bottom left, 21; Joyce Wilson 8 *bottom*, 12 *bottom*.

CLB 2487
This edition published in 1990 by Gallery Books,
an imprint of WH Smith Publishers, Inc,
112 Madison Avenue, New York 10016.
© 1990 Colour Library Books Ltd, Godalming, Surrey, England.
All rights reserved.
Colour separations by Scantrans Pte Ltd, Singapore.
Printed and bound by New Interlitho, Italy.
ISBN 0 8317 6979 3

Gallery Books are available for bulk purchase for sales promotions
and premium use. For details write or telephone
the Manager of Special Sales, WH Smith Publishers, Inc,
112 Madison Avenue, New York, New York 10016 (212) 532-6600.

CONTENTS

INTRODUCTION 4

THE AMERICAN FOREST 6

MOUNTAIN FORESTS 15

THE NORTHERN FOREST 22

EASTERN HARDWOOD FORESTS 26

SOUTHERN BOTTOMLAND FOREST 29

THE FUTURE OF THE AMERICAN FOREST 31

INTRODUCTION

Soon after plants made the transition from sea to land four hundred million years ago, there was pressure through natural selection to grow tall. Green plants depend on photosynthesis to manufacture their food and the elegant strategy of raising leaves skyward allowed plants clear access to light, provided greater leaf surface area and denied sunlight to earthbound competitors. These first primitive trees grew in lowland forests that left the fossil deposits known today as coal.

When the first European explorers landed, they found a continent that comprised a dense, unbroken wilderness extending from the East coast to the Mississippi River. This was in stark contrast to their European homes, where such forests had largely disappeared hundreds of years before. These first explorers did not find virgin terrain, however, since native Americans had already used fire to clear trees for their own purposes.

The earliest Americans, the Indians, led semi-nomadic lives, establishing temporary settlements, hunting the local game until it became scarce and then moving to another area. In contrast, European colonists introduced cereal crops and livestock, which enabled them to live in permanent settlements. The ever-increasing size and sophistication of the colonists' culture made trees indispensable for the lumber and fiber they provided. Such dependence on trees has come at a cost to forests and wildlife. Of the more than 400,000 square miles of virgin forest that once covered the eastern half of the United States, only a tiny fraction remains.

An untouched, mature forest is an intricate community made up of a great diversity of plants and animals. With millions of years to evolve, life in a forest is elaborately interdependent, each organism relying on dozens of others for its existence. Trees depend on fungi to transfer water and nutrients into their roots. Butterflies and bees are required for pollination, while birds and mammals spread the resulting seeds in their droppings, feed on grubs harmful to the tree and use the trunk to store food and to nest.

The Olympic rain forest of western Washington state is a land of giant trees, luxuriant mosses and ferns.

THE AMERICAN FOREST

With the notable exceptions of the West's desert lowlands, the mid-American prairie and the tundra of the extreme north, much of the North American continent is covered by forest. Viewed from space the distribution of trees would appear horseshoe-shaped, arching north up the Pacific coast, across the continent through Canada and down along the eastern half of the United States.

WESTERN WOODLANDS

The mild winters found in the valleys and foothills of California, southern Arizona and New Mexico provide ideal conditions for oak woodlands. The oak woodland community is based upon the annual crop of acorns, an excellent source of nutrition. There are many different types of oaks, both deciduous and evergreen, and they offer a wide variety of nesting, feeding, hiding and hunting sites for wildlife.

Acorn woodpeckers are residents of the oak woodland, where they live in groups of up to sixteen individuals. Rather than migrate after the food supply is depleted, they preserve the yearly avalanche of acorns by storing them in holes they drill in dead trees. These communal storage trees, or granaries, often contain thousands of acorns. The woodpeckers prefer to live in mixed stands of oaks, a strategy which acts as insurance against a failure of one or more of the acorn crops.

The wildlife of a California oak savanna, a place where oaks occur as widely scattered trees on a grassy plain, is especially interesting. Rodents, such as the California ground squirrel, white-footed mouse, Merriam's chipmunk and California pocket mouse, use the grass for food and hiding places. These grassland rodents are hunted by birds, including red-tailed hawks, Swainson's hawks and golden eagles.

Where winters are more severe, such as in the Great Basin of Nevada or the Colorado Plateau of southern Utah and Arizona, a stunted woodland of pinyon pines or junipers becomes dominant. These trees thrive in this harsh environment partly because they have compact leaves formed to cut down the surface area subject to moisture-robbing winds.

Birds like the Clark's nutcracker and the pinyon jay have evolved to take advantage of the nutritious

pinyon pine nut. Nutcrackers have a storage pouch beneath their tongue enabling them to transport dozens of seeds at a time to storage areas. Pinyon jays too can transport many seeds at a time, and a flock of these birds will store millions of pine nuts if they are available.

Like pinyon nuts, juniper berries are nutritious food for wildlife. Animals that eat the red or blue berries benefit both themselves and, because the animals' digestive tract dissolves the protective coat that surrounds the seed, the juniper. Seeds that pass through the digestive tract are much more likely to sprout than ones that simply fall to the ground.

Acorn woodpeckers (facing page top) usually live in groups, sharing common storage trees which can contain up to 50,000 acorns. Facing page bottom: a least chipmunk preparing for the harsh winter of the Colorado Plateau. The red-tailed hawk (above left) is common in woodlands and open country with scattered trees, while the golden eagle (above) hunts in open habitats. The latter forms long-term pair bonds. Clark's nutcracker (left) often breeds early at high altitudes where snow is still deep.

THE PACIFIC COASTAL FOREST

The Northwest coastal forest extends from the outskirts of Anchorage, Alaska, to central California. The coast along this vast distance experiences mild, wet winters and cool, often foggy, summers. Rain falls evenly throughout the year in the north, resulting in the densest growth of coniferous forest in the world, while south from Washington state summers bring prolonged droughts.

Conifers are the dominant trees of the coastal forest and, because the vegetation is less varied and the kinds of food limited, fewer types of animals are found here than in other forest habitats. Seeds, which are contained within the characteristic cone, are the most important source of food, but such things as bark, buds, needles and the cones themselves are eaten as well. Berries, including blackberries, raspberries, gooseberries and others, are also seasonally abundant food. Perhaps surprisingly, mushrooms are an important food source, especially for mammals.

The commercially important salmon leaves the Pacific to swim through the streams and rivers of the coastal forest. Salmon require cold streams with clear gravel beds to spawn and so are particularly hard-hit by clear-cut logging, the commercial harvesting of trees by completely removing large sections of forests. Trees shade streams, keeping the water cool, and preventing the erosion of earth from the riverbanks that silts the river. When a forest is clear cut the shade is removed and winter rains wash large amounts of soil from bare areas into streams, devastating salmon spawning habitat.

Herbivores – animals that live exclusively on plants – are important residents of the coastal forest. Roosevelt elk once roamed widely along the coast, feeding on young trees and underbrush. They prefer the areas where meadow and forest meet, feeding in the meadows and using the forests for shelter and as a place to hide from predators. Occasional herds can still be found from northwestern California to Vancouver Island where, besides man, the primary predator is the mountain lion. Deer, including the mule, the black-tailed, and in southwestern Alaska, the Sitka deer, continue to be common along the coast.

Facing page: (top) fog shrouds Olympic National Park, Washington and (bottom) elk cows and young graze in a meadow. Below: a salmon's view of a coastal forest.

COASTAL REDWOOD FOREST

Old-growth coastal redwood forests, with their massive thousand-year-old trees and fern-covered floors, appear to be left over from an earlier, more primitive time. In fact, the narrow strip of coastal redwoods that remains today is a small remnant of an extensive forest that circled the northern hemisphere millions of years ago. Coastal redwoods require the high humidity, moist soils and moderate temperatures that are limited to the coastal fog belt of central California into southern Oregon. Fog, which condenses on the needles and falls as drops at the base of the trees, contributes several inches to the average sixty inches of precipitation that fall on the redwood forest.

It is easy to be overwhelmed by the size of old-growth redwood trees, which can grow to heights in excess of 300 feet, and to overlook the wildlife that live among them. The California slender salamander is an amphibian, a land animal which lacks lungs and must absorb oxygen through its damp skin. It hides within the moist litter of the forest floor until it rains and then emerges to hunt insects and worms. Banana slugs, close relatives of snails, also thrive in the forest floor, leaving a trail of slime as they crawl.

The Pacific shrew is a tiny, nocturnal predator of the redwood forest floor. Shrews have very high metabolic rates and must eat more than their weight in food each day. They paralyze their prey, such as worms and insects, with venomous saliva and store the food in their dens. They sleep during the day, awakening frequently to snack on these stored foodstuffs.

The California slender salamander (below) thrives in the moist understory of the redwood forest. The banana slug (bottom) is a giant relative of the common snail. The hole or stoma behind its head is for breathing. Facing page: shafts of sunlight piercing fog in the coastal redwood forest.

Western Old-Growth Forests

In the Pacific Northwest, old-growth forests are havens for wildlife. In an undisturbed forest, trees such as Douglas fir grow to be giants, reaching nearly 300 feet in height, with many of the trees more than 200 years old. Inevitably, some of the trees will succumb to insects, disease, weather or fire, leaving behind dead snags that may stand for many decades, providing habitat for many different species.

The pileated woodpecker is an important excavator of cavities in old-growth forests. For its nest it requires large snags in which it shapes large hollows with rectangular openings. Eventually the holes become home to mammals such as flying squirrels, pine martens and bushy tailed woodrats.

Great horned owls (right) are widely distributed throughout North America's forests. They hunt rabbits, rodents and even other owls. Below: a wood duck, a true forest bird.

Water birds such as the wood duck and common merganser, as well as owls like the great horned, use larger natural cavities that are common in old-growth snags. The endangered spotted owl depends on large, old trees to nest and the uncluttered understory of old forests to hunt. Clear-cut logging of forests removes their preferred nesting sites and replaces the clear understory with dense second growth. Larger mammals like raccoons, spotted skunks, gray foxes and bobcats also use cavities to escape bad weather or for breeding.

Large fallen logs are also characteristic of old-growth forests and add to the diversity of this forest's wildlife. The sheltered areas beneath the logs are used as cover by creatures like the blue grouse. Birds such as the winter wren and various flycatchers use the bare branches as perches, while hollow logs provide den sites for black bears.

The great gray owl (left) favors dense coniferous forests. It is the largest North American owl. Below: a resting black bear sow and her wide-awake cub in their hollow tree den.

MOUNTAIN FORESTS

Since the mountain ranges of the west, notably the Sierra Nevada, Cascades and the Rockies, intercept moist air masses as they move eastward from the Pacific Ocean, they are far wetter than the surrounding lowlands. These highlands are dominated by conifers, trees that are well adapted to the extremes of temperature and water availability found here.

The Appalachian Mountains of the east are notable for their diversity of plant life. These mountains are older than their western counterparts and, in their more inaccessible areas, their remaining primeval forests suggest how the virgin forest that once covered the eastern half of the United States must have looked.

Conditions in mountain environments becomes more extreme with increasing elevation; snowfall is heavier and lingers longer and the growing season is shorter. In the northern latitudes, the combination of long, severe winters and a short growing season results in similar conditions. The timberline of mountains and the northern extent of trees in the Arctic represent the failure of trees in the face of increasing cold.

Facing page: a rain-swollen tributary enters the Matanuska River, Alaska. Right: Whitewater Falls in the North Carolina Appalachians and (below) the Great Western Divide of the Sierra Nevada seen from Sequoia National Park.

MOUNTAIN FOREST BIRDS OF PREY

The intertwined branches of a mountain forest make rapid movement difficult. Some types of animals are excluded from this three-dimensional maze, but others are very well adapted to it. A group of hawks, which includes goshawks, as well as sharp-shinned and Cooper's hawks, are at home hunting in mountain forests. These birds have slim bodies, short wings and rudder-like tails which make them ideally suited to the quick moves required to hunt forest life.

The northern goshawk prefers mixed stands of hardwoods and conifers of boreal and mountain forests. It can take prey as large as rabbits, but mainly feeds on smaller mammals, like red squirrels, or other birds, such as grouse and crows. It uses its long tail and rounded wings to maneuver quickly and to avoid obstacles.

The uncommon Cooper's hawk is found throughout forests of the United States. It hunts by dashing through woods in a low, swift flight as it dodges trees and brush. To brake and steer, the Cooper's hawk uses its tail, which is nearly as long as its body. It will not tolerate the smaller sharp-shinned hawk, excluding it from its woodlands. The sharp-shinned is especially skillful at plucking small birds out of the air or from twigs.

Below: the large, telescopic eyes of a Cooper's hawk and (facing page) a low flying northern goshawk.

GREAT SMOKY MOUNTAINS

Never disturbed by ice age glaciers, the forests of the Great Smoky Mountains, located in the southern Appalachian Mountains in eastern Tennessee and western North Carolina, are among the most ancient in North America. Yet these ancient forests are just remnants of much more widespread forests once found throughout the eastern United States. Characterized by a long growing season, generally mild temperatures, abundant moisture and rich soils, the Great Smoky Mountains have forests of deciduous trees on the lower slopes and coniferous trees at higher elevations.

A common resident of the Smokies is the black bear, the smallest and most widely distributed of the North American bears. As true omnivores – animals that eat almost anything – they feed on berries, honey and roots, as well as on small rodents and carrion. While black bears do retreat to dens for a winter's sleep, they do not hibernate in the strict sense. Their temperature, breathing

Right: the haze that gives the Great Smoky Mountains of Tennessee their name. Below: a black bear and (below right) fall in the Great Smoky Mountains.

and heartbeat remains more or less normal throughout the winter, allowing them to wake and forage during particularly mild winters.

The northern saw-whet owl, a nocturnal bird of dense woods, is also a resident of the Great Smoky Mountains. The saw-whet mostly eats insects, but will also eat mammals such as mice and young flying squirrels. Its name comes from its call which is reminiscent of the sharpening of a saw blade.

Below: a northern saw-whet owl in its nesting cavity.

ANCIENT TREES

High in the western mountains, where poor soil, little moisture and penetrating winds combine in one of the least hospitable environments imaginable, grows the bristlecone pine, the oldest living species of tree. These are short, squat trees sculpted by nature into fantastic shapes. They grow slowly, adding as little as one inch to their diameter in a hundred years. The oldest of these patriarchs, which are more than 4,500 years old, appear to be mostly dead, bearing only small tufts of living needles.

Though not the oldest, at nearly 3,000 years, nor as tall as the coastal redwood, the Sierra Nevada's giant sequoia is the biggest, having the greatest volume of any tree found in the United States.

Sequoias depend on fire for their continued well being. Fires cannot penetrate the thick, insulating bark of the sequoia, but they do remove competing evergreens and leaf litter, leaving a thin layer of nutrient-laden ash. The heat of the fire dries cones held high in mature trees, allowing the seeds to fall after the fire into soil that is perfectly prepared and free from competition.

Above: the eroded base of an ancient bristlecone pine. Bristlecone pines (below) eke out an existence at altitudes in excess of 11,000 feet. Pine trees reproduce via seed-containing cones (below right). At an estimated age of 2,700 years, the Grizzly Giant (facing page) in Yosemite National Park's Mariposa Grove is one of the oldest giant sequoias.

THE NORTHERN FOREST

The immense northern or boreal forest stretches over the North American continent from the Alaskan interior across northern Canada to the Great Lakes and on to New England, extending south along the Appalachian Mountains as far as Tennessee. It is a belt of conifers about 500 miles wide that separates the arctic tundra to the north from the mixed forests to the south.

Three pines – the red, the eastern white and the jack – dominate the boreal forest. Two other major conifers, black and white spruces, are important as well. Stands of quaking aspen mingle with needle-bearing trees, temporarily holding their own until eventually losing out to the conifers.

WILDLIFE OF THE NORTHERN FOREST

Beavers are the northern forest's engineers, building dams with tireless energy and great precision. The dams are vitally important for the ponds that they form, as these ensure a protective moat around the underwater entrance to their home, or lodge. The dams are often elaborate affairs which begin with the beaver poking sticks into the mud bottom of a running stream. Wood is

gradually added until it forms a barricade from bank to bank. To stop the inevitable flow through the interwoven sticks, the beaver adds mud taken from the pond bottom.

The chief dam construction materials – poplar, aspen, willow, birch and maple – are also the beaver's favorite foods. As their front surfaces coated with hard enamel, a beaver's teeth are well suited to felling trees. The teeth never stop growing, relying on their constant use to keep them the proper size.

Moose, the world's largest living deer, range throughout the boreal forest. They are generally solitary but will gather at shallow ponds, lakes and rivers where they eat willow and aquatic plants, their preferred food. Being so large, a healthy adult moose is safe from most predators except grizzly bears and wolves, which will take young and sick animals.

The impressive antlers of the bull moose begin to grow in April, attaining full size by August. They are shed between December and February. The antlers are used to thrash brush, probably to mark territory, and for occasional battles during the rut, though threat displays usually suffice.

Porcupines have defensive barbs called quills which are an effective defense against just about any animal that threatens them. In fact, more than simply discouraging predators, quills can be lethal weapons – lodged in the tongue or mouth they can become such an impediment that the animal so injured may starve. Porcupines strip the bark off trees and eat the soft layer beneath it. They also eat herbs, mistletoe, pine needles and rodents.

Even porcupines are no match for the fisher, a weasel-like animal that eats porcupines and nearly anything else it may come across. These nimble, tree-dwelling mammals inhabit the boreal forest across Canada and range south along the major United States mountain ranges.

Wild dogs like the red fox and coyote are found throughout the boreal forest where they eat rodents and other small mammals. The gray or timber wolf roams far and wide over the boreal forest and northern tundra. Outside of Alaska, the timber wolf exists in the United States in significant wild populations only in Minnesota and Michigan's Isle Royale National Park.

Facing page: (top) a beaver dam revealed by melting snow and (bottom) a resting bull moose. The gray wolf (top left) may hunt by day or night in packs formed mainly of family groups, while the nocturnal red fox (left) hunts alone.

23

WILDLIFE OF THE FAR NORTH

After enduring the winter in the northerly part of the boreal forest while feeding on lichen found on south slopes where the snow is thinnest, barren ground caribou move over age-old routes to their calving grounds along the Arctic coast. They spend the winter in separate groups, the bulls alone together and the cows with their calves and yearlings, but in the spring the ages and sexes coalesce. There are no staging grounds where the animals assemble; small groups simply unite as they approach the historic migratory routes, eventually forming northward-moving living streams.

Barren ground caribou are masters of survival in this harsh environment. As they trek north, they travel on firm snow and the ice of lakes and rivers, avoiding thickets where wolves may hide. Once free of the forest, they continue in a direct course over the featureless tundra, feeding as they go. Their insulating coat is made of air-filled hollow hairs which also add buoyancy as they swim across rivers in their path.

The Porcupine caribou herd, named for the Porcupine River, ends its journey in late May on the narrow coastal plain of Alaska's Arctic National Wildlife Refuge. The herd exceeds 150,000, with as many as 40,000 caribou cows arriving to feed and give birth. The North Slope is almost a desert and the precipitation that does fall in late May or June usually falls as snow, saving the newly born calves from soaking rains. In addition, the debilitating Alaskan mosquitoes become plentiful weeks later here than in the forest.

Thousands of calves are born, all within a week, and their numbers swamp potential predators such as wolves, wolverines, golden eagles, barren ground grizzlies and Arctic foxes. To further insure their survival, caribou calves mature quickly. Within a week the calf can keep up with its mother; within two weeks it can outrun a wolverine or grizzly.

Caribou spend the summer feeding on lichens, mushrooms, grasses and other green plants. Birch and willow twigs, and even dropped antlers, are also eaten. By August the caribou have put on the fat that they will need to see them through the approaching winter. By September most have left the coastal plain and are heading south, back to the shelter of the forest.

Caribou are North America's wildebeest, and their huge migratory numbers attract the tundra's version of East Africa's predators. Notable among these is the gray or timber wolf, the arctic equivalent of the leopard. Once more widespread, gray wolves still inhabit Alaska, much of Canada, northern parts of Minnesota, Wisconsin and Michigan and a few may be found in Montana and perhaps Idaho.

Gray wolves are social animals that mate for life and live in packs comprised of four to seven family members. They inhabit territories of from forty to one thousand square miles. The strongest, or alpha, male is normally the leader and the entire pack contributes to raising his young.

Wolf packs are major predators of hoofed mammals such as deer, moose, elk and caribou. Like most predators, the prey taken by wolves are the young or infirm. The replacement of the native bison and elk with cattle and sheep resulted in the widespread killing of wolves at the turn of the century. Today, in addition to rancher concerns about wolf predation on domestic animals, wolves are killed in Alaska to increase moose herd sizes. The effectiveness and ethics of wolf-control programs are subject to continuing controversy.

Though they are the same species, wolves are separated into different races. The Arctic, or white wolf, is limited to the remote and desolate Canadian islands above the Arctic Circle where its prey includes musk oxen and arctic hares.

Below: the antlers of a caribou bull. Facing page: (top) a pack of timber wolves and (bottom) a herd of Alaskan caribou.

EASTERN HARDWOOD FORESTS

Emerging south from the boreal forest in the lower elevations of New England, on into Ohio and further south to Arkansas and Oklahoma, is the vast central or eastern hardwood forest. More than forty different tree species are found here, most of which are deciduous. In the northern part of this forest, sugar maple and beech are common, while in the central portion oaks and hickories can be found. Sycamore, tulip poplar, sweet gum and several types of pine are characteristic of the southern part. Only one tree, the white oak, is found throughout the entire area.

The huge crop of leaves each autumn is the basis of the mixed deciduous forest ecosystem. Fungi and bacteria are the primary decomposers, attacking the fallen material and breaking it down with special enzymes. Earthworms also feed directly on the leaves of several species of trees. Insects, in turn, feed on the fungi, and beetles, such as the eastern eyed click beetle, prey upon the insect larvae. The moist habitat created by the rotting leaves is home to more varieties of salamander than any other forest in the world.

A common resident of the eastern forest, the wild turkey is the largest American game bird. After roosting in trees each evening, wild turkeys actively forage on the ground for seeds, nuts, acorns and insects. They lay their eggs on the ground in a simple leaf-lined scrape or a natural depression in the ground. Predators, such as opossums, snakes, crows and coyotes, eat the eggs but the adult turkey is an able defender and uses deception to lead potential enemies away from the nest.

Above: fall oak leaves that will soon add to the litter on the forest floor, where the slender salamander (below) thrives.

Above: the American toad, a woodland resident. Once eliminated from much of its range, the wild turkey (below) has been reintroduced into many areas.

The woodchuck is commonly found in the northeastern woods, south to Louisiana and eastward to the Atlantic Ocean. Unlike so many other forest species, it actually expanded its range as the eastern forest was cut down from the eighteenth century onwards. Originally strictly a forest dweller, the woodchuck moved into the cleared areas and acquired the name groundhog.

After feeding and growing fat all summer, woodchucks retire to their den when the weather turns cold. They are true hibernators, slowing down their body processes during the long winter's sleep, breathing only once every few minutes and allowing their body temperature to fall dramatically.

Compared to the western United States, the east has fewer small mammals. One that occurs in great numbers, however, is the eastern chipmunk, which is found in every state east of the Mississippi River, except Florida. Like the fourteen species of chipmunks that are found in the western United States, the eastern chipmunk's food consists largely of seeds, berries, nuts and vegetable matter. Food is stored temporarily in their ample cheek pouches, which can hold impressive amounts.

The southern flying squirrel is found in eastern forests from the Mississippi River east to the Atlantic Ocean. Its name is misleading; the flying squirrel doesn't fly, it glides using side flaps of skin that stretch between its front and rear legs. Being a light animal, with its skin flaps pulled tightly, it can float for a distance of more than a hundred feet using its tail for directional control.

SOUTHERN BOTTOMLAND FOREST

Throughout much of the United States, rivers cut a fairly narrow path as they race toward their destinations. But the rivers of the central South's Gulf plain cut a more leisurely swath as they pass over a land whose slope is nearly imperceptible. These rivers easily jump their banks, flooding the surrounding land and creating the distinctive southern bottomland hardwood forests of the region between Texas and northern Florida.

This is a complicated environment; a mixture of land that is nearly always dry with land that is usually wet. The resulting forest, which includes cottonwood, yellow poplar, sycamore, swamp maple and many others, is a place often difficult for man to visit but truly a haven for wildlife.

Some of the bottomland forest wildlife can be intimidating. Snakes are common and, although their bite is seldom fatal, cottonmouths can be disturbingly abundant in damp places. The name comes from the light "cotton" lining of their mouth which is exposed while gaping at an intruder. This is also a home to the American alligator, the largest reptile found in North America. Once alligators were hunted for their hides and were much reduced in numbers. Now protected, they are gaining in numbers in some areas.

Other bottomland wildlife is more familiar and far less intimidating. Wood ducks, true forest dwellers, are common, and tricolored heron and bitterns can be found too. The anhinga, a diving bird, is often seen holding its wings out to dry, and mammals such as the mink and the muskrat also make their homes here.

Facing page: special prop roots supporting an Everglades tree and (top) a tricolored heron hunting for fish. As it lacks oil glands to waterproof its feathers the anhinga (above) must dry its wings after diving for fish. Below: the American alligator, the largest reptile in North America.

FOREST FIRES

With the first forest, inevitably, came the first forest fire. People often view fire as merely destructive, seeing it as wrecking valuable stands of timber, torching homes and terrorizing wildlife. But fire predates our settlements as well as our economic interests and has a genuine place in the way forests work.

Fires are natural disruptions, killing some trees, damaging others, and removing the layer of litter that builds up on the forest floor. The aspen, pitch pine, jack pine and lodgepole pine depend on fire to provide the bare soil and full sunlight they require. Under normal conditions jack pines retain their cones which remain tightly closed. When heated by a fire the cones open, dropping huge quantities of seeds on the ash-covered ground. With fresh seeds and little competition, the jack pine seedlings thrive.

Aspen trees are opportunists, growing quickly after a part of the forest floor has been cleared by fire, logging or avalanche. They react so quickly because of their ability to sprout from underground roots which are protected from most calamities. In fact, without the disturbance of a

---

Yellowstone National Park's summer-long fires of 1988 destroyed many years' worth of accumulated forest litter.

forest fire, aspen is usually overgrown by longer-lived, more shade-tolerant conifers such as Douglas fir or Englemann spruce.

The fast-growing "suckers" that sprout after an aspen stand has been removed by fire or logging provide nutritious browse for moose, elk and mule deer. As the trees grow they become important to beavers, which prefer immature trees of around two inches in diameter for constructing their dams and lodges.

The red-cockaded woodpecker depends on fire to maintain the open mature pine woodland that it prefers. It nests in holes that it bores in pines infected with heart fungus. As a result of fire suppression and the logging of immature trees, the red-cockaded woodpecker is threatened with extinction.

As the Yellowstone fires of the summer of 1988 revealed, excluding fire from many American forests over extended periods of time is both impossible and usually self-defeating. The summer-long fires were a natural disaster on the scale of a hurricane or an earthquake, but they were not an environmental disaster. The raging crown fires that destroyed the familiar groves of old-growth lodgepole pine and spruce fir were in part a result of a policy which suppressed fires – the accumulated fuel added to the destruction. The fires changed the Yellowstone ecosystem, reconstituting it in ways that only time will reveal.

THE FUTURE OF THE AMERICAN FOREST

The forests of America are a resource for both humans and wildlife. The industrial forester views the natural forest as inefficient, preferring one comprised of a single, commercially valuable tree species. This simplified forest is undoubtedly more vulnerable to such things as acid rain and excludes any species of wildlife that depends on older trees.

As the American forest has been depleted, so have the animals that depend so completely upon it. The spectacular ivory-billed woodpecker was lost to the conversion of southeastern old-growth pine forest to commercial stands. Uncounted salmon once returned to rivers along much of the west coast to spawn. Hydroelectric dams, poor logging practices and pollution have severely reduced their numbers. As the old-growth forest of the Pacific Northwest is further reduced, the spotted owl may become the next casualty.

The interdependence between forest and wildlife is most clearly illustrated by the mountain lion. Also known as the panther, cougar or puma, this magnificent cat was once found in almost every forest of the western hemisphere. No other mammal, with the exception of man, was as widely distributed in the American wilderness. It is now dramatically reduced throughout much of its range, especially in the east. A subspecies of the mountain lion, the Florida panther, once ranged

Acid rain may have caused the destruction of a Smoky Mountain forest (above). Below: a mountain lion.

widely throughout the South. Habitat destruction has forced the panther out of all but a few swamps of southern Florida and only a critical few remain.

Evergreen and deciduous trees mix in the forest above Zion Canyon in Zion National Park, Utah.